CAFFEINE
✚
CHUTZPAH

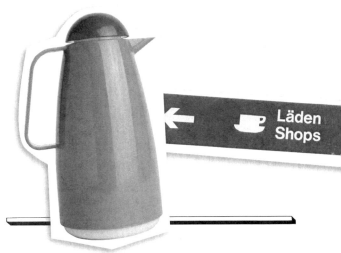

Läden
Shops

Steven Case

THE
PILGRIM
PRESS
Cleveland

This series is dedicated with respect, admiration, and gratitude to the youth of the Windermere Union Church who allowed me to try out many of these lessons in our meetings. Thank you. You made me better.

The Pilgrim Press, 700 Prospect Avenue, Cleveland, Ohio 44115-1100
thepilgrimpress.com
© 2008 by Steven Case

Scripture quotations, unless otherwise noted, are from the New Revised Standard Version of the Bible, © 1989 by the Division of Christian Education of the National Council of Churches of Christ in the United States of America and are used by permission. Changes have been made for inclusivity.

All rights reserved. Published 2009.

14 13 12 11 10 09   5 4 3 2 1

Library of Congress Cataloging-in-Publication Data

Case, Steve L., 1964-
  Caffeine and chutzpah / Steven Case.
     p. cm.
  ISBN-13: 978-0-8298-1844-4 (alk. paper)
  1. Bible--Biography--Study and teaching. 2. Youth--Religious life--
Study and teaching. 3. Christian life--Study and teaching. 4. Church
work with youth. I. Title.
  BS605.3.C37 2009
  268'.433--dc22

                        2009005366

CONTENTS

DAA-DEEE DAA-DEEE

THEME: GOD
ORDER HERE

God. The beginning of all things. Before there was anything—ANNN-EEE-THIIINNG— there was God. God is the alpha and omega (the beginning and end) and is generally a nice supreme being all around. In this lesson we will look at different aspects of God's character. Who is God? What is God? Where does God get off telling me how to run my life?

START THINKING

True or False?

- God is the Father Almighty.
- God is the Mother of all creation
- God made the rose but Satan made the thorn.
- God knows what my great-great-granddaughter will name her pet kitten.
- God is an old white man with a voice like James Earl Jones. He wears a long blue robe, sits on a throne, and has a bucket of lightning bolts on one side and a bucket of blessings on the other.
- God likes pie.
- God listens to some prayers and ignores others.
- God made people because he was lonely.
- God made the earth in six days and then took a nap.
- God is like Santa for grown ups.

TABLE NOTES

In the space below or on a napkin or the back of a place mat, draw a picture of what you thought God looked like when you were a child. Then draw a picture (or symbol) of what you think God is now.

Is it necessary to teach children about a "physical being" God who has fingers and toes and teeth and other human characteristics? What has changed about how you visualize God? Was there something specific that changed your mind?

SCRIPTURE MENU

Look up one or more of the sets of verses, and respond to the discussion questions that follow.

Genesis 3:8 (NRSV)
They heard the sound of the Lord God walking in the garden at the time of the evening breeze, and the man and his wife hid themselves from the presence of the Lord God among the trees of the garden.

If God is "walking" and can feel "the evening breeze," can we assume that God is a physical being?

Singer Joan Osbourne posed the question, "What if God was one of us / Just a slob like one of us / Just a stranger on a bus / Trying to make his way home?" Start by answering the question in all its possibilities. Then ask, "Why is God trying to make his way home?"

Read Genesis 2:5–7.

Do you personally prefer to imagine God as an "ethereal" sort of spirit being or a God with dirt under his fingernails? Explain your own answer but also see if you can explain the other.

Read Exodus 3:13–15.

Moses asks God, "Who do I say sent me?" God responds, "Tell them I AM sent you." This is as close as we're likely to get to God's name without a face-to-face meeting. The phrase "I AM" in Hebrew looks sort of like this: YHWH. Even though some believed this was the "name that should not be spoken," it was eventually pronounced YAH-wey.

The following passages all contain images of God in the "feminine" sense. Read the scriptures and talk about the possibilities of God as our Mother.

Isa. 42:14

Isa. 49:14–15

Isa. 66:12–13

These passages contain images of God doing tasks that would (at the time) be described as women's work.

Ps. 22:9–10a, 71:6

Isa. 66:9

Lk. 13:18–21, 15:8–10

These passages contain images of God as a female bird protecting her young.

Deut. 32:11–12

Ps. 17:8; 36:7; 57:1; 91:1, 4

Isa. 31:5

This verse has an image of God as a mother bear.

Hosea 13:8 (NRSV)
I will fall upon them like a bear robbed of her cubs,
 and will tear open the covering of their heart;
there I will devour them like a lion,
 as a wild animal would mangle them.

There are several verses, such as Deuteronomy 4:24, that describe God as a jealous God. Psalm 86:15 portrays God as being slow to anger. Ephesians 1:7-8 is about God's forgiving grace.

In what ways do you understand your parents better now than you did as a child? How is our relationship with God like that?

If we are often at our best when things are at their worst...if we continuously grow and learn and get better at what we do (both as a species and individually)...*and* if we are made in the image of God...is it unreasonable to say that God grows, learns, practices, continues to create, gets happy and sad, and has any other human characteristics? Explain.

TAKE HOME BAG

*David used the Hebrew words **Chay-Elohim** to describe God. Write down ten words to describe what you feel like after a ride on a rollercoaster or at the end of a rock concert and you'll get David's sense. Pray to THAT God this week.*

TIP

I am plenty safe enough in his hands; I am not in any danger from that kind of a Deity. The one that I want to keep out of reach of is the caricature of him which one finds in the Bible.

—Mark Twain

IS IT HOT IN HERE OR IS IT JUST YOU?

THEME: SATAN

Disclaimer: The goal of this and every Exploration is to spark discussion. I want you to think, to have an opinion, and to talk about it with others. You can skip this Exploration if you think it is too hot to handle (pun intended). But we encourage you to let the discussion flow, even when it might be uncomfortable. That's how we learn.

ORDER HERE

After Satan's resurgence in the 1970s movie *The Exorcist*, he has taken a back burner (pun intended) over the last few decades. Your belief or doubt about Satan and his power (or lack thereof) is entirely between you and God. There are some who say that the Satan in the scriptures is merely an allegory or a personification of our doubts and temptations. Others can't seem to even get through a church service without at least one reference to a guy dressed in red with horns and carrying a pitchfork. In this Exploration we look at how Satan is portrayed in the scriptures. Is "the devil" an actual being?

START THINKING

Choose one.

If I get an F on the test, it's because

- My teacher is Satan.
- God is mad at me.
- Satan tempted me with video games.
- I didn't study.

If I smoke weed, it's because
- Satan tempted me.
- I'm an idiot.
- I have to work on my self-confidence.

If highjacked planes fly into buildings, it's because
- Madmen took them over to make people afraid.
- Satan wanted it to happen.
- God wasn't paying attention.

If hurricanes hit the East Coast it's because
- God was upset about Disney offering benefits to same-sex partners.
- Satan wanted to see what would happen.
- Weather conditions permitted.

TABLE NOTES

In the space below, in your journal, or on the back of a place mat, draw a long and winding road that disappears off into a distant horizon. At the end of that road, so far you can barely see it, draw a dream or goal that you have in your life (career, sports car, college education, house). Now draw a block in the center of the path.

What is the block made of? _____

How large did you draw it? _____

Give it a name. _____

What's keeping you from that goal at the end of the road?

_____

How many blocks do you think you will encounter?

_____

The word Satan comes to us from the Hebrew *ha-satan*, which literally means "stumbling block."

When something is in your way, are *you* most likely to

- Go over?
- Go around?
- Go through?
- Go home?

Scripture Menu

Have someone read aloud Job 1:6–12 and ask the questions aloud.

Satan (the character) is not God's equal; he is God's servant (albeit a mouthy one). Satan cannot exist without God's permission. Why do some people have to have a villain? Is everything black and white, right and wrong?

If we removed the idea of Satan as the ultimate evil, what would happen to Christianity?

Notice how God does not seem all that upset by Satan's presence here. Other translations say, "Where have you been?" or "What are you doing here?" Think of all the different ways your mother could say, "What have you been up to?"

In Hebrew, "Satan" can mean "the accuser," and in some translations he's referred to as the "Designated Accuser." Do you have someone in your group that seems to be the designated singer? The designated brain? The designated pessimist?

Read Matthew 4:1–11 and then ask the questions.

In this story, Satan goes right to Jesus's sense of identity. "You think you're all that? Trust me your not." When do you tend to let voices of doubt in your own head get the better of you?

Who is the "voice" in your life that would be most likely to say to you, "You're not so much." (You can include yourself in that.) If it's someone close to you, why do you hang out with that person?

Mark 8:32–33 (MsgB)
He said this simply and clearly so they couldn't miss it. But Peter grabbed him in protest. Turning and seeing his disciples wavering, wondering what to believe, Jesus confronted Peter. "Peter, get out of my way! Satan, get lost! You have no idea how God works."

Why do you think that Jesus identified Peter with Satan?

Think about what Jesus was about to do. How easily distracted are you from homework? Jesus was about to die because God asked him to. Would you be tempted to say "No"?

TAKE HOME BAG

Go back to your drawing in Table Notes of the obstacle in your path. Write down three ways (large or small) you can start to go over, around, or through that obstacle this week.

 TIP

If you can't stand the heat, get out of the kitchen.

MADE FOR EACH OTHER

THEME: ADAM AND EVE

ORDER HERE

You are a by-product of your history. Generations of your family have led you to be what you are. Generations of people you have never met have led you up to this moment. Adam and Eve did not have these issues. Before them, there were no people, no rules, no long-held traditions. It was all new to them. Each thing they did was by their own choice. Often we start to blame our parents or our past for our current situation, yet God has given us the choice to live in the past or to start something new.

START THINKING

For the following statements, write down a number from 1 to 10, with 1 meaning "strongly disagree" and 10 meaning "strongly agree."

- We are the products of a guiding hand but not necessarily as we find it in the book of Genesis.
- If my parents say "don't touch this" it's pretty much an invitation for me to go and touch it.

- If I could be who I am and erase all of my memories and start completely clean—fresh, with a complete do over—I would go for it.
- If a product says "New," I'd probably try it because it's new.
- If a product says "Improved," I'll probably buy it and find out how it's different.
- The whole creation story is one I've always had a problem with.
- If God wants to speak to me through the creation story, God will. I don't need to buy into the whole thing.
- God created me. That doesn't mean I have my entire life laid out for me. I will be who I want to be.

TABLE NOTES

Consider five objects that are on the table or on a nearby counter. (If you are in a classroom, use objects in the room.) Write down a new name for each object. Imagine you have never seen it before. What are you going to call it?

SCRIPTURE MENU

Look up one or more of the sets of verses, and respond to the discussion questions that follow.

Genesis 1:24–27
Genesis 2:4–7

The Bible contains two accounts of the creation story. If you have time, read them both and compare them. How are these two passages different?

Adam was aware of two things—the world around him at the present moment and God. How would your personal world change if you focused on those two things? What if you dropped the baggage of your past and stopped fussing about the future?

Genesis 2:20–23

Do you think there is one person out there who is made for you? Does God pick out the people we will spend the rest of our lives with? Would that make it easier?

God made Eve and brought her to Adam. What if instead of searching for "Mr./Ms Right" we simply chose to "be" right ourselves? Do you think God would bring someone to you?

God said it wasn't right for Adam to be alone. Do we need to think that you need others to complete you? To make you whole?

Who has the right to say whether or not something made by God is not amazingly wonderful? Perhaps a better question is who do we *give* that right?

Here's a hard question: If God is "Three in One" (Father, Son, and Holy Spirit)—and God is, was, and always will be—then when God made Adam in the image of God, how did the Son and Holy Spirit play a part in that creation?

1 Corinthians 15:44–49

This passage seems to suggest a difference between the body and the soul. As if they are two different things.

Where did "first man, Adam," come from? According to the other verses, where did his soul come from?

The "last Adam" will be from body to soul instead of the other way around. Who is the "last Adam"?

"We will also bear the image of the man of heaven." How can we do that?

Read Psalm 8:3–6.

In this reference to Adam from the Psalms, David tells us that we are God's favorite creations. It also gives us responsibility for God's creation. If it's ours, why do we spend so much time asking God to fix it?

Do you take the story of Adam and Eve literally? Why or why not?

What is the major lesson from this story? Are there many lessons?

For generations, people have used the idea that Adam was created first to advocate men's power over women. Which part of the story could be used for those purposes?

TAKE HOME BAG

Fill this week with "firsts." Let today be the first time you try a food that you've never tried. Take a different path to your classroom for the first time. Speak to someone new for the first time. Keep a record and see how many "firsts" you can accomplish before the next meeting.

TIP

The person you are right now...is the person that you have chosen to be.

SO LET'S JUST GO LIKE THIS
(RIGHT ARM, LEFT ARM, TURN AROUND, NOD YOUR HEAD)

Theme: ABRAHAM

Order Here

Besides having a goofy camp song written about him, Abraham is named in the scriptures as "the father of multitudes." Yet he didn't start being a father until he was in his nineties. God saw Abraham (then going by the name Abram) and decided this was the one he wanted to use. He showed Abraham the night sky and said, "See the stars? That's how many descendants you'll have."

Start Thinking

True or False?

- When I pack a suitcase I make a list and make sure I have everything I need before I even start loading the suitcase.
- I love spur-of-the-moment road trips.
- I want to grow up, get married, have kids, raise them in a good place, get a job I enjoy, and live a completely ordinary and honorable life.
- I could pack up and be ready to leave my house for a weekend in fewer than 10 minutes.

- I could pack up and be ready to leave my house for a year in less than a day (including stopping mail and notifying school and friends).
- If I had to be ready to leave my life and never come back to it—not tell anyone or pack a bag, just simply go—I could go.

TABLE NOTES

Using the space below or a napkin or the back of a place mat, see how many stars you can draw in 60 seconds. Wait for your teacher to say "Go."

What would you say if someone told you this was going to be the size of your family?

SCRIPTURE MENU

Have someone look up the verses and ask the questions aloud.

Genesis 12:1–4 (NRSV)

¹**Now the Lord said to Abram, "Go from your country and your kindred and your father's house to the land that I will show you.** ²**I will make of you a great nation, and I will bless you, and make your name great, so that you will be a blessing.** ³**I will bless those who bless you, and the one who curses you I will curse; and in you all the families of the earth shall be blessed."**

⁴**So Abram went, as the Lord had told him; and Lot went with him. Abram was seventy-five years old when he departed from Haran.**

In packing up and leaving, Abraham wasn't just doing what God told him to do. He was defying all the expectations of his family. He could have stayed but he didn't. Have you ever defied expectations?

If someone were to ask your parents what they "expect" of their children, what would they say?

Read Genesis 18:1–15.

Visitors tell Abraham that Sarah will have a baby. And Sarah laughed. This is one of those "God-can-do-anything-because-God-is-God" verses. What would you need before you believed God was actually speaking to you?

Have you ever been dwelling on a problem and then when you turn on a radio the song is speaking directly to what you've been going through? Is it reasonable to think that God had a hand in that? Why or why not?

Read Genesis 22:1–10 and answer the questions.

This is probably one of the most heart-wrenching scenes in the Bible. God calls on Abraham to do something horrible. Abraham is fully prepared to do it. God knows from the beginning that he will bless Abraham for his obedience. But Abraham doesn't. Was this unreasonable for God to ask?

Can you think of a time in your life when you were going through your own version of Hell and then later on something good happened because of it?

Could you work as a secret service agent or some other profession where you might have to kill or be killed for the president?

Read the next three passages and then discuss them together.

Genesis 25:7–11
Genesis 16:15
Genesis 21:9–13

Isaac and Ishmael—do you know where that story is today? Look at the news or pick up a newspaper. What is going on between Israel and the rest of the Middle East right now?

All that started with these two sons of Abraham. If you could do something that you knew would have an effect a thousand years from now, what would you do?

What if you didn't get to plan it ahead of time? What if someone offered to show you how your last major decision is going to affect the planet in a thousand years? Good or bad, would you want to know?

Romans 4:2–5 (MsgB)

If Abraham, by what he did for God, got God to approve him, he could certainly have taken credit for it. But the story we're given is a God-story, not an Abraham-story. What we read in Scripture is, "Abraham entered into what God was doing for him, and *that* was the turning point. He trusted God to set him right instead of trying to be right on his own."

If you're a hard worker and do a good job, you deserve your pay; we don't call your wages a gift. But if you see that the job is too big for you, that it's something only *God* can do, and you trust him to do it—you could never do it for yourself no matter how hard and long you worked—well, that trusting-him-to-do-it is what gets you set right with God, *by* God. Sheer gift.

The Message translation says that Abraham "entered into" what God was already doing for him. Do you think God is already doing something for you? What keeps us from entering into what's already going on?

Take Home Bag

James 2:23 talks about Abraham's faith, that it was a blend of faith and action. This is how he earned the label "God's Friend." Think of one or two ways you can earn that same label this week.

TIP

If you can do it and you do it and get paid...that's a job. If you can't do it and you do it anyway...that's a gift.

PUT 'IM ON A CAMEL'S BACK AND SEND 'IM OFF TO UR

Theme: DANIEL

Order Here

The video series "Veggietales" made cute the story of Daniel, with music worthy of Andrew Lloyd Weber. But deep within the story of Daniel we find a man with *cajones* of steel. Daniel had an incredibly close relationship with God. God spoke with Daniel because Daniel spoke with God. Daniel made prayer a priority—not just a priority but a fixation. He was fervent in his prayer time and this made him open to what God had to say.

Start Thinking

True or False?

- I can watch TV, listen to music, talk on the phone, and do my homework all at the same time.
- My mother/father never has to repeat herself/himself.

- I rarely remember my dreams.
- I can remember some dreams that I had when I was a little kid.
- I have had nightmares from which I wake up screaming.
- I pray every day (beyond grace at supper and before going to bed).
- I enjoy prayers that are written out for me like poetry (such as The Shield of St Patrick).
- I can stand up and pray off the cuff without problem.
- God wants us to use proper language when we pray.
- There is an acceptable prayer position.
- People who pray five times a day while facing Mecca are just taking it too far.
- God speaks to everyone.
- God speaks to me.

TABLE NOTES

In the space below or on a napkin or the back of a place mat, draw a bizarre creature that is part jungle animal, part bird, and part human. Then draw a vision from one of your own dreams that you haven't been able to shake.

Now read Daniel 7:1–8.

SCRIPTURE MENU

Read or look up one or more of the verses, and respond to the discussion questions that follow.

Daniel 2:8–11 (NRSV)

⁸The king answered, "I know with certainty that you are trying to gain time, because you see I have firmly decreed: ⁹if you do

not tell me the dream, there is but one verdict for you. You have agreed to speak lying and misleading words to me until things take a turn. Therefore, tell me the dream, and I shall know that you can give me its interpretation." ¹⁰The Chaldeans answered the king, "There is no one on earth who can reveal what the king demands! In fact no king, however great and powerful, has ever asked such a thing of any magician or enchanter or Chaldean. ¹¹The thing that the king is asking is too difficult, and no one can reveal it to the king except the gods, whose dwelling is not with mortals."

Do you believe in fortunetellers? People on TV who claim they talk to the dead? Have you ever had your Tarot cards read? Are these things possible?

Do you like magic shows? Do you prefer big illusions like David Copperfield creates or more in-your-face magic like David Blaine?

Why do people believe in psychics?

Daniel 2:14–18 (MsgB)
When Arioch, chief of the royal guards, was making arrangements for the execution, Daniel wisely took him aside and quietly asked what was going on: "Why this all of a sudden?"

After Arioch filled in the background, Daniel went to the king and asked for a little time so that he could interpret the dream.

Daniel then went home and told his companions Hananiah, Mishael, and Azariah what was going on. He asked them to pray to the God of heaven for mercy in solving this mystery so that the four of them wouldn't be killed along with the whole company of Babylonian wise men.

Notice in the story that at no time does Daniel ever take credit for what he is saying. Have you ever gone into a situation and simply acknowledged that you were in over your head and prayed that God would give you the words?

Daniel also takes time out to pray with his friends (even as the executioner is sharpening his ax). Have you ever prayed with someone else (outside of church)? Have you ever been on a youth event and stood around a candle holding hands and "felt" the difference in a collective prayer? Talk about that.

What's the closest thing we have to a prophet today?

If someone showed up and announced, "God is speaking through me," what do you think would happen in your church?

Daniel had a habit of saying "No" to power if it conflicted with his beliefs. *Read Daniel 1:7–13 or 4:19 or 6:10.*

How well do you say "No" to power—not just to be a pain in the butt but when you really believe something is wrong?

If your boss said you could take office supplies from work, would you?

If your boss asked you to lie to a client on the phone, could you?

Have you ever written a letter to the editor or signed a petition? About what?

Why is what is "right" often what "hurts"?

Have you ever been a part of a group that suddenly decided "he" or "she" was not welcome in the group anymore? Did you follow the group?

Take Home Bag

Make a commitment to pray. Perhaps every night on your knees beside your bed. You don't need to recite something unless that makes you feel connected. Just talk to God. Say another prayer before your feet touch the floor every morning. See if you feel any different by the next meeting.

Tip

When you wish upon a star, your dreams come true.

—Jiminy Cricket, "When You Wish Upon a Star"

HAND ME THE
ROYAL BINOCULARS

THEME: DAVID

ORDER HERE

Why don't the Sunday School take-home papers ever show David hacking off Goliath's head with his own sword and then carrying it around for a few weeks? David was all over the board with God. He was chosen (anointed) by God to be king when he was just a little kid. He killed the giant, was a street corner musician, danced nearly naked at the head of a parade, committed both adultery and murder, hid the ark of the covenant (that gold box from the Raiders movies), and wrote some of the coolest song lyrics ever. He wept in God's presence and danced there too. How can you be this scattered on the "Bible Heroes" map and still make the list of God's favorite sons?

START THINKING

Choose one.

- I tend to pray most when I'm on top of the world / when I'm lying in a puddle in a filthy parking lot (metaphorically speaking).
- I prefer Shakespeare / Green Day.
- When my soul is filled with JOY, I will usually dance / sing / paint / shout.
- When I have created a hole for myself so deep I can't see the surface, I blame someone else / get out by any means necessary / get out (by climbing) / call for help.

TABLE NOTES

In the space below or on a napkin or the back of a place mat, draw small circle. Draw four or five rings around that circle.

Put a dot on the ring that you think represents how close the following people were/are to God.

Moses	Jesus
David	Your youth pastor
The President	

SCRIPTURE MENU

Look up the verses and ask the questions that follow.

1 Samuel 16:23 (NRSV)
And whenever the evil spirit from God came upon Saul, David took the lyre and played it with his hand, and Saul would be relieved and feel better, and the evil spirit would depart from him.

1 Samuel 18:5–11 (NRSV)
⁵David went out and was successful wherever Saul sent him; as a result, Saul set him over the army. And all the people, even the servants of Saul, approved.

⁶As they were coming home, when David returned from killing the Philistine, the women came out of all the towns of Israel, singing and dancing, to meet King Saul, with tambourines, with songs of joy, and with musical instruments. ⁷And the women sang to one another as they made merry,

"Saul has killed his thousands,
 and David his tens of thousands."

⁸Saul was very angry, for this saying displeased him. He said, "They have ascribed to David tens of thousands, and to me they have ascribed thousands; what more can he have but the kingdom?" ⁹So Saul eyed David from that day on.

¹⁰The next day an evil spirit from God rushed upon Saul, and he raved within his house, while David was playing the lyre, as he did day by day. Saul had his spear in his hand; ¹¹and Saul threw the spear, for he thought, "I will pin David to the wall." But David eluded him twice.

If it happened a first time, wouldn't you get the hint to leave? This was David in his glory days. People danced for him and sang songs about him.

How does leadership act when new leadership comes in? Have you ever been the "out with the old" or the "in with the new"? Talk about that.

How well does your church accept change? (Ask your youth minister about spears.)

2 Samuel 12:20 (MsgB)
David got up from the floor, washed his face and combed his hair, put on a fresh change of clothes, then went into the sanctuary and worshiped. Then he came home and asked for something to eat. They set it before him and he ate.

This was David at his lowest. He had slept with another man's wife, had her husband killed, and was lying on the floor weeping. What was the lowest you've ever been? Talk about a time when you felt so far from God you wondered if God was even there.

How long do you stay down when you are down? Where does the resolve to stand up and keep going come from? (You don't have to answer "God" just because it's a church thing.)

Read one or more of the following: Psalms 32, 38, 41, 46, 51, 69.

These are some great examples of David's all-over-the-board lyrics. Read any of these Psalms out loud, but don't think of them as fluffy poetry. Think of them as if they were punk lyrics, or songs sung by an old blind bluesman in a smoky New Orleans bar.

When you feel "low," how much do you need someone around you saying, "It's okay—things will get better—the sun will come out tomorrow"?

When you are down, do you listen to sad music or happy music? Are there songs that make you turn up the radio in the car and put the windows down?

Are there songs that seem to reach into your heart and rip it out of your chest?

Read Psalm 28.
This is probably the greatest example of David feeling both "up" and "down" in the same psalm. (It was probably written about the time his son died.) Notice that his "life-in-the-puddle" feeling did not include questioning God's existence. David believed that God was there...with him...all the time.

Take Home Bag

Go back to the circles you made in Table Notes. Draw a small circle (with your initials in it) somewhere on one of the rings. How close do you feel to God today? Make a note to come back to this Exploration every few weeks and see how your "closeness" changes.

Tip

Dance like there's nobody watching.

WISEGUY

THEME: SOLOMON

ORDER HERE

Here's a little known fact: the "s" in the word "shazam" stands for Solomon—the one character in the word that is not from Greek mythology and not a physical trait for Captain Marvel. Impressed? You should be! It's one of those little tidbits that will make you look smart...like Solomon. Solomon was one of David's offspring. Besides being smart he was also a hopeless romantic. Apparently a little sweet talk will get you 700 wives and 300 concubines. And apparently that many wives and concubines can bring about the downfall of your kingdom. It's a wonder he had time to do all that writing. The Song of Solomon and the books of Proverbs and Ecclesiastes are all attributed (almost in their entirety) to King Solomon.

START THINKING

Score each statement from 1 to 10, with 1 meaning "strongly disagree" and 10 meaning "strongly agree."

- Those who walk with their nose in the air are more likely to trip on something.
- People with one face can see where they are going. People with two faces constantly look behind them.
- When life is a hurricane, a fat wallet isn't going to hold you down.
- Decency is a life jacket. Nastiness is a bowling ball. Let's go swimming.
- He that dies with the most toys...still dies.

- Rumors and gossip build walls. Truth is a bulldozer.
- Truthfully, when too many cooks actually work together, they can make a really good soup.
- Give away your only ice cream cone and you'll get a bigger one free!
- Hog it to yourself, and it will fall in the dirt.
- Life is a gumball machine. The righteous get their favorite color. The nasty lose their nickel.
- No matter what you might think, God knows and he will do something about it.
- Beauty mixed with bad judgment is like piercing a frog's ass with diamond stud.
- A good life is like a never-empty box of hot donuts.
- A bad life is like a short hair in your salad.

TABLE NOTES

Imagine God comes to visit you and says, "I will give you one thing. You name it. I will give it to you. No questions asked. What'll it be?" In the space below or on a separate sheet of paper, draw a picture or a symbol.

When you are done, read 1 Kings 3:1–14.

SCRIPTURE MENU

Look up one or more of the sets of verses, and respond to the discussion questions that follow.

Ecclesiastes 3:1–8 (NRSV)
¹**For everything there is a season, and a time for every matter under heaven:**
²**a time to be born, and a time to die;**
a time to plant, and a time to pluck up what is planted;
³**a time to kill, and a time to heal;**
a time to break down, and a time to build up;
⁴**a time to weep, and a time to laugh;**
a time to mourn, and a time to dance;
⁵**a time to throw away stones, and a time to gather stones together;**
a time to embrace, and a time to refrain from embracing;
⁶**a time to seek, and a time to lose;**
a time to keep, and a time to throw away;
⁷**a time to tear, and a time to sew;**
a time to keep silence, and a time to speak;
⁸**a time to love, and a time to hate;**
a time for war, and a time for peace.

Solomon knew about the seasons (planting and harvesting), he knew about birth and death. He understood that there was nothing that could be done to stop this process or change it. It was going to happen. Look at the other unchangeable/unstoppable items in this list. Can you give a specific example for each, either in our own culture or in your own life?

1 Kings 7:7 (MsgB)
He built a court room, the Hall of Justice, where he would decide judicial matters, and paneled it with cedar.

John 10:22–24 (NRSV)
²²**At that time the festival of the Dedication took place in Jerusalem. It was winter,** ²³**and Jesus was walking in the temple, in the portico of Solomon.** ²⁴**So the Jews gathered around him and said to him, "How long will you keep us in suspense? If you are the**

Messiah, tell us plainly."

Acts 3:11 (NRSV)
While he clung to Peter and John, all the people ran together to them in the portico called Solomon's Portico, utterly astonished.

Acts 5:12 (MsgB)
Through the work of the apostles, many God-signs were set up among the people, many wonderful things done. They all met regularly and in remarkable harmony on the Temple porch named after Solomon.

Years ago, the porch (sometimes called a portico) was the deciding feature on many houses. It was a place of belonging where arguments were settled, lemonade was sipped in the cool of the evening, and the breeze was appreciated. Did you have a front porch growing up? Maybe you used to hang out on a balcony. Where was the place that you and your friends or your family or people in your community could come and just hang out and talk?

Does this element of life still exist?

What would happen if we built a porch on every government building in the world?

Take Home Bag

Just this once, you can go back and change your Table Notes answer if you want to.

Tip

Pick up the book of Proverbs. It's full of them.

A SPIRITUAL DOPE SLAP

Theme: JOB

Order Here

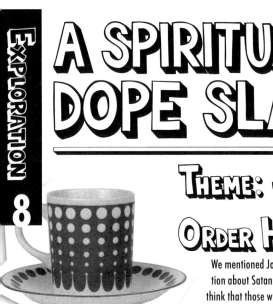

We mentioned Job in the Exploration about Satan. We like to think that those who experience suffering on the level that Job did somehow deserve it—that it is was justified. But Job was a good guy. Respected in his community. A good father. He had earned what he had and was respectful to God. Yet in this story he is, metaphorically, placed on the floor of life's outhouse. Many of us get a parking spot too far from the entrance to the movie theater, and we think, "God must be mad at me today." The speeches at the end of the book of Job—Job's rant and God's response—are the stuff of legend.

Start Thinking

Choose one.

- I would be most upset if I lost my ride home / homework / cell phone.
- If I find a five-dollar bill on the ground, it means God loves me / I'm lucky / somebody else is having a bad day.
- I prefer jigsaw puzzles / Sudoku / crosswords.
- If I pull into a parking spot and the radio is playing a song I like, I will get out of the car and get on with my day / wait for the song to finish.
- God watches us from heaven with a stack of lightning bolts / buckets of blessings / a look of complete amusement.

- God already knows what my great granddaughter will name her kitty / what I'm about to circle on this page / that it's all up to me.
- Who let the wild ass go free? God / Me / The author of this book / Old McDonald

TABLE NOTES

In the space below or on the back of a place mat, write down something that would just ruin your day. Then pass your book or paper to someone else and have that person write something that would make your situation just a little bit worse. Repeat the process until everyone has had a chance to write on everyone's book or paper.

SCRIPTURE MENU

Look up the verses and ask the questions that follow.

The difference between a rhetorical question and a literal one is this: a rhetorical question isn't meant to get an answer but to get a reaction. If your mother says "Do I look stupid to you?" DON'T ANSWER! That's a rhetorical question. God's response to Job's rant is a series of rhetorical questions. Did you put the stars in place? Did you make an ocean? Did you make a hippopotamus? (Seriously—see Job 40:15.) All of these God brings up, not to get an answer but to get a reaction.

Can you think of some ways that we as a species tend to play God?

At the time, people said of the Titanic, "Even God couldn't sink this ship." Were we moving too far too fast?

Is there anything that you think is too far into God's territory (such as gene splicing or creating a superconductor)?

God gave us these brains and abilities: shouldn't we use them?

Have you ever listened to an elementary school student complain about the amount of homework? Have you ever sweated working outside for a day and then listened to someone indoors complain about how hot it was? Do you think God feels this way? Explain.

Job 39:5 (ASV)

Who hath sent out the wild ass free? Or who hath loosed the bonds of the swift ass?

God was trying to explain that humanity may have the ability to take away a wild animal's freedom and make it a farm animal, but only God can give freedom. Can you give away someone else's car? How is this the same thing?

Was there ever a time when someone had to sit you down and tell you, "Here's the way it is, kid."

When and for what was your last dope slap?

Job 2:11 (NRSV)

Now when Job's three friends heard of all these troubles that had come upon him, each of them set out from his home—Eliphaz the Temanite, Bildad the Shuhite, and Zophar the Naamathite. They met together to go and console and comfort him.

Job's three friends all came when they heard he was in trouble. Notice that they didn't try to fix his problem (at least not right away); they just sat with him for seven days. Talk about a time when someone tried to jump in and fix your life and you just wanted someone to listen.

Why do we have trouble letting someone feel bad? How quickly do you get tired of pity?

Job 40:3–5 (NRSV)

3Then Job answered the Lord:
4"See, I am of small account; what shall I answer you?
I lay my hand on my mouth.
5I have spoken once, and I will not answer;
twice, but will proceed no further."

Job 42:1–6 (NRSV)

1Then Job answered the Lord:

²**"I know that you can do all things,**
and that no purpose of yours can be thwarted.
³**'Who is this that hides counsel without knowledge?'**
Therefore I have uttered what I did not understand,
things too wonderful for me, which I did not know.
⁴**"Hear, and I will speak;**
I will question you, and you declare to me.'
⁵**I had heard of you by the hearing of the ear,**
but now my eye sees you;
⁶**therefore I despise myself,**
and repent in dust and ashes."

These last passages are two of the most important parts of this chapter. They show that Job finally gets the idea that God is God and he is not. Why is this hard for some people?

In what ways do we put God in a box?

We see images of God in cartoons, Sunday school papers, and movies, and he is usually an old white guy (though Morgan Freeman was pretty cool in the role). Is it wrong of us to make these assumptions? How then can we teach about God? If Jesus called God "Daddy," shouldn't that be good enough for us?

Why do we have to touch it, taste it, smell it, hear it, or see it in order to fully believe? What is faith? Is that difficult?

If we must see, hear, taste, touch, and smell in order to believe, why would God put himself beyond these? Are our senses limitations to connecting with God? Explain.

Take Home Bag

Take a look at Job, chapter 39. Create your own question from God to Job. Write it down and then use it this week as a screensaver, or put a note on your mirror.

It's a great big universe and we're all really puny. We're just tiny little specs about the size of Mickey Rooney.

—Wako, Yako, and Dot.

YOU TALKIN' TO ME?

THEME: BALAAM

ORDER HERE

The story of Balaam could be a spin-off of the Ten Commandments. Just before Moses died and the Israelites crossed into the Promised Land, there was a king named Balak who saw the Israelites in his land as an infestation. So he called a professional curse-bringer (Balaam) to get rid of his problem. At first Balaam refuses. The king asks again, and Balaam agrees (this is where the talking donkey comes in). God decides to send Balaam to the king with a message. After multiple worship services to the king's god, Balaam relays God's message and the king gets ticked off and they part ways. Balaam now takes his role as God's prophet seriously but still can't keep himself out of trouble via sex and money. This lesson deals with the first part of the story. If you want the second part, you'll have to go look it up yourself.

START THINKING

*Let's pretend we're casting a movie called **Balaam**. Read the descriptions and write down who you think should play the part and why.*

Balaam: Should be good looking and charismatic (there will probably be a scene with the sexy Moabite women in the film). Should have good range. Can bless Israel or curse them. Should be able to play off the donkey well.

Balak: The bad guy. He's got an ulterior motive and his only goal is to get this guy Balaam to bring down a curse upon these people who are infesting his land. And he knows Balaam's one weakness: money.

The Angel: Not the cherub with the harp and the fluffy wings. This is God's warrior angel. Big. Brandishes two swords.

The Voice Of The Donkey: This can be played as comic relief (à la Eddie Murphy) or more like a Jiminy Cricket role.

Sexy Moabites: Choose at least two actors/actresses to play the parts of a church that seduce Balaam into a sex-as-worship church service.

TABLE NOTES

Draw a picture of a treasure chest. Make it as detailed as you want. Just draw it closed and locked. When you are done, stare at the picture you've drawn. In your imagination, think of your greatest treasure (literal or figurative) inside the treasure chest.

SCRIPTURE MENU

Look up one or more of the sets of verses, and respond to the discussion questions that follow.

Numbers 22:5–7 (NRSV)

⁵He sent messengers to Balaam son of Beor at Pethor, which is on the Euphrates, in the land of Amaw, to summon him, saying, "A people has come out of Egypt; they have spread over the face of the earth, and they have settled next to me. ⁶Come now, curse

this people for me, since they are stronger than I; perhaps I shall be able to defeat them and drive them from the land; for I know that whomsoever you bless is blessed, and whomsoever you curse is cursed."

⁷So the elders of Moab and the elders of Midian departed with the fees for divination in their hand; and they came to Balaam, and gave him Balak's message.

Consider a woman who says she is a Christian Tarot card reader. She believes God gave her the "sight," and she does readings for people. Do you think this is possible? Can you use any profession for God? Can you be a Christian hit man? A Christian stripper?

Why do we tend to think that God would call only the "happy happy joy joy" Christians to do his work?

Would God speak to just anybody? Would God call on an abusive radio DJ and say, "I want you to deliver a message for me?" Would God ask you? Why or why not?

The whole story of Balaam and his talking donkey is too long to reprint here. Check it out in Numbers 22: 121–35.

The donkey sees the angel even when Balaam does not and tries do veer off to the side of the road. This happens three times, and Balaam nearly kills the donkey. How many times do you need a clue before you get a dope slap? Have you ever been given a spiritual dope slap?

Why do you think that Balaam isn't all that shocked to hear a talking donkey but an angel of God puts him on his knees?

It's hard to know why God was angry at Balaam when God was the one who gave permission for Balaam to go. Some scholars have theorized that Balaam (based on past and future behaviors) wasn't going for God's purposes but for the money. What is the most important part of doing mission work for you? Do you come to church to be social or to be close to God or a combination of several things? Did motivation make a difference in your answers to the earlier question about jobs?

Notice that Balaam's major problem with the incident is that he was embarrassed in front of the king's messengers. Pride seems to be a thing with Balaam. Was this one reason God used a donkey to teach him a thing or two?

This is just something to wonder about: We know that Satan could have been one of God's angels. Satan's name means "stumbling block" or, in some cases, "adversary" or "one who stands in the path." What was the angel of God doing in this story? Hmm. Wouldn't that be interesting?

2 Peter 2:15–16 (KJV)

15Which have forsaken the right way, and are gone astray, following the way of Balaam *the son* of Bosor, who loved the wages of unrighteousness;
16But was rebuked for his iniquity: the dumb ass speaking with man's voice forbad the madness of the prophet.

Peter would have known the books of the Old Testament by heart. He spoke of Balaam as an example of bad behavior. Has your mother or father ever brought up an older family member or friend who screwed up and used that story to teach you a lesson about something? That's what Peter was doing. Despite following God's order and being a prophet for him, Balaam apparently earned the reputation of turning people away from God and following the wrong path again and again.

If the path is straight and we're walking a crooked line, do you think God will try to keep us on the path or use us whenever we cross paths? What is it off to the side—"Ooo, shiny"—that usually diverts your attention?

Take Home Bag

Perhaps the greatest lesson we can learn from Balaam's life is that where your treasure is, there is your heart. Go back and look at your treasure chest. Do you need to swap out the contents? Think of way to do that this week.

Tip

God will speak to us in one of two ways. He will whisper in your ear or smack you upside the head with a brick. Listen for the whisper. The brick hurts. Every time.

—Al Sterling

HOOK, LINE, AND SINKER

THEME: JONAH

ORDER HERE

What happens when you disagree with God? To say "God agrees with me" is presumptuous. But to hear God as clearly as you hear a voice on the radio and then to say, "Nah, I don't think so," can get you in trouble. Jonah was called by God to a specific task. Jonah was blinded by his own hatred for the Ninevites. God sent a storm and then a fish, and Jonah got the point. He did what he was told. He still wasn't happy about it, but he did what God told him to do.

START THINKING

After each statement, write down a number from 1 to 10, with 10 meaning "Absolutely" and 1 meaning "I'm outta here."

- If God told me to put all my change for the year in a Salvation Army kettle, I would.
- If God told me to skip one meal a week and put the money into a Feed-the-World charity, I would.
- If God told me to wash my neighbor's car and accept no money to do so, I would.
- If God told me to wash the car of the person in my school who hates my guts, I would.
- If God told me to wash the car of the person in my school who hates me the most and I said "No" and then got four flat tires, THEN I would go and wash the car.
- If God told me to be a minister, I would.
- If God told me to be a trapeze artist, I would.

TABLE NOTES

In the space below or on the back of a place mat, make a list of people you'd like to see get a "life ticket"—a financial penalty for doing something stupid. Examples include texting while driving and screwing up your drive-thru order. These can be funny or serious.

SCRIPTURE MENU

Have someone look up the verses and ask the questions aloud.

Jonah 1:1–2 (NRSV)

¹Now the word of the Lord came to Jonah son of Amittai, saying,
²"Go at once to Nineveh, that great city, and cry out against it;
for their wickedness has come up before me."

Shouldn't that be enough? God says, "Go," and we go. Right? What would it take for you to believe that God was actually speaking to you?

Have you ever been thinking about a problem and then get in the car and have the song on the radio speak directly to that problem? Is this God or coincidence? Why would it be hard for some people to believe it's God answering them?

Jonah 1:3 (NRSV)

But Jonah set out to flee to Tarshish from the presence of the Lord. He went down to Joppa and found a ship going to Tarshish; so he paid his fare and went on board, to go with them to Tarshish, away from the presence of the Lord.

Where do you hide when you know your parents are looking for you? Does "hiding" always have to be physical? What are some ways that we hide ourselves from one another and from God?

Jonah 1:4–7 (NRSV)

⁴But the Lord hurled a great wind upon the sea, and such a mighty

storm came upon the sea that the ship threatened to break up. ⁵Then the mariners were afraid, and each cried to his god. They threw the cargo that was in the ship into the sea, to lighten it for them. Jonah, meanwhile, had gone down into the hold of the ship and had lain down, and was fast asleep. ⁶The captain came and said to him, "What are you doing sound asleep? Get up, call on your god! Perhaps the god will spare us a thought so that we do not perish."

⁷The sailors said to one another, "Come, let us cast lots, so that we may know on whose account this calamity has come upon us." So they cast lots, and the lot fell on Jonah.

Jonah 1:12–15 (NRSV)

¹²He said to them, "Pick me up and throw me into the sea; then the sea will quiet down for you; for I know it is because of me that this great storm has come upon you." ¹³Nevertheless, the men rowed hard to bring the ship back to land, but they could not, for the sea grew more and more stormy against them. ¹⁴Then they cried out to the Lord, "Please, O Lord, we pray, do not let us perish on account of this man's life. Do not make us guilty of innocent blood; for you, O Lord, have done as it pleased you." ¹⁵So they picked Jonah up and threw him into the sea; and the sea ceased from its raging.

Jonah 1:17 (MsgB)

Then God assigned a huge fish to swallow Jonah. Jonah was in the fish's belly three days and nights.

Despite all the evidence provided by Sunday school take-home-papers, the Bible never says "whale"—only "huge fish." Storytellers like the image of Jonah sitting there like Geppetto from the Pinocchio movie. Jesus later quotes this verse in reference to himself. The Bible does say that Jonah was "digested" for three days and that the fish "vomited" him up onto dry land.

Read Jonah 3:1–10.

God wanted "repentance" from the people of Nineveh. This usually requires atonement, sorrow, contrition, and some regret. How did the people of Nineveh show this to God?

Have you ever wronged someone and gotten away with a half-hearted "Sorrrry"?

What if your apology included atonement, sorrow, contrition, and regret?

Imagine you are supposed to meet some friends at a grocery store parking lot and then go to the movies instead. You are the one with the car. If you forget or you show up at the wrong grocery store, what would you do to make it up to your friends? If you were one of those stuck in a parking lot, what would you expect?

The people of Nineveh fasted and dressed in burlap to show God they were sorry. It was an outward sign of something internal, like wearing black to a funeral. Can you think of a modern day "sign" like this?

Read Jonah 4:1–11.

Jonah felt more pity for the tree than he did for the people of Nineveh. He was more upset that the tree died than he was at the near death of a city. What causes people to be so selfish? Where do our beliefs about other people come from?

When the planes hit the World Trade Center, hate crimes against Muslims skyrocketed. Do we ever have the right to say "God doesn't love you because..."? Does anyone have that right? *Go back to Table Notes and put your own name on your own list. How does that feel?*

Take Home Bag

Somewhere there is someone to whom you still owe an apology. Somewhere there is someone who is still hoping for your forgiveness. Think of one thing (large or small) you could do this week to make both of those happen.

Tip

Do not tell fish stories where the people know you; but particularly, don't tell them where they know the fish.

—Mark Twain

GOOD GIRLS DON'T

THEME: MARY

ORDER HERE

When we talk about Mary, we have a tendency to picture a little Midwestern girl in an outfit her mother sewed for the Christmas pageant. Usually she's in blue and white. She has a plastic doll from the church nursery wrapped up in an authentic pre-Caesar teddy-bear blanket. The lights are dim, you can smell candles and hay. The whole congregation thinks, "Awwww." In truth, though, there is something heartbreaking about Mary. Girls her age in the time and the place where she grew up would have been told the stories about the Messiah. They would have been taught the prophecies. Even when she was actually sitting in a pile of hay holding a brand new baby, somewhere in the back of her mind she would have known how it was going to end. And she did it all anyway.

START THINKING

Imagine Hollywood is making a new Jesus movie.

Mary's costume should be _____.

The best actress to play Mary would be _____.

A rock song that could be renamed "Mary's Theme" is

_____.

If the movie were set in modern times, the location would be

_____.

And Mary would have a job as _____.

A movie about Mary should be called _____.

TABLE NOTES

List ten things you think are typical of all teenage girls regardless of class, location, or upbringing.

_____

_____

_____

_____

_____

_____

_____

_____

_____

_____

SCRIPTURE MENU

Read or look up one or more of the verses, and respond to the discussion questions that follow.

Luke 1:28–36
Luke 1:46–56 (NRSV)

Mary was probably no older than you. More than likely, hers was an arranged marriage, but that was common in those days. Think of your list of things typical to a teenage girl and to the list for Mary add "brave." She utters what is probably the most profound phrase in the Bible: "I am the Lord's servant."

Could you have said "yes"? Seriously, if you saw an honest-to-God angel who said, "Guess what? It's YOU!" would you have said, "Yes"? What if it weren't a choice? What would your reaction be?

What would you have told your parents? Would they have believed you? If you are a guy, imagine what your parents would say if you said, "My girlfriend is pregnant." Would you have believed your girlfriend when she said, "It was the Holy Spirit"? Joseph apparently did not (which is understandable). Then an angel appeared to Joseph and said, "Yeah, it's true" Then immediately you have to pack up and move to your father's home town because the government said so.

Luke 2:34–35 (NRSV)

³⁴Then Simeon blessed them and said to his mother Mary, "This child is destined for the falling and the rising of many in Israel, and to be a sign that will be opposed ³⁵so that the inner thoughts of many will be revealed—and a sword will pierce your own soul too."

Up until this point Luke's gospel was all about Joy. Then Mary is told (just eight days after Jesus was born) that she was going to feel like she'd been pierced with a sword. Have you ever lost someone close to you? Broken up with a longtime boyfriend/girlfriend? How does it feel physically?

The ancient Jews believed that different parts of the body were responsible for different emotions. The stomach was where love came from (no, not the heart). When you love someone you feel all "squooshy"; when you lose that someone it's like a kick in the stomach. Is it fair for God to ask a girl to carry that kind of burden? If any of it had happened any other way, do you think you would be sitting here right now?

John 19:25 (MsgB)

Jesus' mother, his aunt, Mary the wife of Clopas, and Mary Magdalene stood at the foot of the cross.

Mary was right there beside her son when he breathed his last. Can you think of the worst pain you've ever been through? How do you move on? Imagine you could have taken that weeping 40-something woman in your arms at that moment. What would you have said?

TAKE HOME BAG

Go around the circle/table and have each person bring up a current issue in the world, community, or your school. Have each person say, "I am the Lord's servant."

When you gather together next time, talk about how it felt and if you did anything servant-like this week.

Mary, Did you know that your baby boy has walked where angels trod? And when you kiss your little baby, you kissed the face of god.

—Mark Lowry

LOCUST MUFFINS

Theme: JOHN THE BAPTIST

Order Here

You know that one friend you have... the one with the mouth? Everyone has at least one friend who just can't seem to keep his or her mouth shut at the right moment. When the teacher says, "Do I look stupid?" there's always that one person who breaks into a sweat and you literally have to clamp your hand over their face to keep them from laughing out loud. At the same time, these are usually the most passionate people you know. They'd be willing to get in trouble for a cause they believe in.

John the Baptist was one of these people. He was also Jesus' cousin. He was one who went around saying, "Something very, very big is coming." Like a biblical hurricane warning, John spoke out to everyone and ticked off the people who were most in the position to make him stop.

Start Thinking

True or False?

● Buttons, T-shirts, yard signs, and the like are all vital parts of any political campaign.

● Bumper stickers can influence opinion.

● In these days of 24-hour news cycles, the press can make an "issue" out of anything.

- In these days of 24-hour news cycles, the press *should* make an "issue" out of *anything*.
- I can say "no" to power.
- I have been known to get in trouble for my opinions.
- We should remove all the table and chairs from the lunchroom to see if it would cut down on the unofficial class system that occurs in high school.
- Being of age to vote is more important to me than being of age to drive or to drink

TABLE NOTES

In the space below or on a napkin or the back of a place mat, draw a picture of a T-shirt. Now create a design that you think would most get you in trouble if you wore it to the White House (or maybe to a church board meeting). Remember, including profanity is uncreative—you can do better than that.

SCRIPTURE MENU

Look up one or more of the sets of verses, and respond to the discussion questions that follow.

Luke 1:13–15 (ASV)

¹³**But the angel said unto him, Fear not, Zacharias: because thy supplication is heard, and thy wife Elisabeth shall bear thee a son, and thou shalt call his name John.** ¹⁴**And thou shalt have joy and gladness; and many shall rejoice at his birth.** ¹⁵**For he shall be great in the sight of the Lord, and he shall drink no wine nor strong drink; and he shall be filled with the Holy Spirit, even from his mother's womb.**

What does the Holy Spirit feel like?

Have you ever stood on your chair at the end of a concert? Have you ever felt that right-place-right-time feeling as you drove along with the windows down? Maybe it was the last night of a mission trip, maybe it was when you were on a roller coaster. What does that feel like physically? Mentally? Emotionally?

What would it be like to feel that all the time? How would people treat you?

Read John 1:16–18.

Luke 3:8–9 (MsgB)
"It's your *life* that must change, not your skin. And don't think you can pull rank by claiming Abraham as 'father.' Being a child of Abraham is neither here nor there—children of Abraham are a dime a dozen. God can make children from stones if he wants. What counts is your life. Is it green and blossoming? Because if it's deadwood, it goes on the fire."

The Jewish people believed they were already "in" as far as heaven goes. In this passage from Luke, John was saying there's more to it than just being "in" because you are one of the "chosen." You have to back it up with actions, share what you have (Luke 3:10–11), and repent (Matthew 3:1–2). "Repent" means "to atone," "to show some sincere regret," "to make it up to the one you wronged," and then to turn around and not do that anymore.

John 1:19–28 (NRSV)
[19]This is the testimony given by John when the Jews sent priests and Levites from Jerusalem to ask him, "Who are you?" [20]He confessed and did not deny it, but confessed, "I am not the Messiah." [21]And they asked him, "What then? Are you Elijah?" He said, "I am not." "Are you the prophet?" He answered, "No." [22]Then they said to him, "Who are you? Let us have an answer for those who sent us. What do you say about yourself?" [23]He said,
"I am the voice of one crying out in the wilderness,
'Make straight the way of the Lord,'"
as the prophet Isaiah said.
   [24]Now they had been sent from the Pharisees. [25]They asked

him, "Why then are you baptizing if you are neither the Messiah, nor Elijah, nor the prophet?" ²⁶John answered them, "I baptize with water. Among you stands one whom you do not know, ²⁷the one who is coming after me; I am not worthy to untie the thong of his sandal." ²⁸This took place in Bethany across the Jordan where John was baptizing.

Luke 3:19–20 (NRSV)
¹⁹But Herod the ruler, who had been rebuked by him because of Herodias, his brother's wife, and because of all the evil things that Herod had done, ²⁰added to them all by shutting up John in prison.

John had no problem telling it like it was. And it got him in trouble. Can you name one or two people in our culture who do this? Do you know someone like this?

What usually keeps us from speaking up in situations where power is abusing the people?

Now read Mark 6:17–29.

TAKE HOME BAG

Jesus called John "a shining light." John was also called "a voice in the wilderness" and "thunder in the desert." In what way could you be any one of these three this week?

TIP

Brood of snakes! What do you think you're doing slithering down here to the river? Do you think a little water on your snake skins is going to make any difference?

—John The Baptist

Your type really makes me puke, you vacuous coffee nosed melodious pervert!

—Graham Chapman, Monty Python's Argument Clinic

YEAH? ARE YOU GOING TO STOP ME?

Theme: THE OTHER MARYS

Order Here

Mary of Magdela is probably one of the most undeservedly maligned characters in the Bible. For centuries she was considered a prostitute (and still is in some circles). The truth is, she was nothing of the kind.

There was a Pope in the year 591 who preached that several of the "Marys" found in the four gospels were, in fact, all the same person. Mary (Martha's sister) may have been the woman who anointed Jesus feet. These multiple Marys had a profound impact on Jesus' ministry, but there is nothing in the scriptures to make us think all references to "Mary" are to the same person.

Start Thinking

Would you rather...

- Watch a surgeon at work / Watch a minister at work.
- Fish / Cook fish.
- Change a diaper / Change a tire.
- Lead a mission trip / Fund a mission trip.
- Defy authority / Defy tradition.
- Wear a school uniform / Wear an outfit that people will laugh at.
- Get in line / Sneak in the back without paying.
- Be wrong / Be right and be called a liar.

TABLE NOTES

In five words or fewer, write down the primary message Jesus wanted to share.

_____

_____

_____

Now write down ten qualifications you would have to have in order to be able to share it.

_____

_____

_____

_____

SCRIPTURE MENU

Have someone look up the verses and ask the questions aloud.

Luke 8:1–3 (NRSV)

¹Soon afterwards he went on through cities and villages, proclaiming and bringing the good news of the kingdom of God. The twelve were with him, ²as well as some women who had been cured of evil spirits and infirmities: Mary, called Magdalene, from whom seven demons had gone out, ³and Joanna, the wife of Herod's steward Chuza, and Susanna, and many others, who provided for them out of their resources.

There's an old saying, "The two most fragile things in the world are a young woman's reputation and a young man's ego." Do you think this is true?

Has anyone ever believed a complete lie about you?

When was the last time you were expected to do what was expected of you? Is there a time to shut up and do it?

Jesus' ministry was a well-funded machine. It would appear that Mary of Magdela and some other women helped fund it out of their own pockets. Is there any "cause" that you give money to? If you have no money, is there a ministry you would give your time to?

Luke 10:41–42 (NRSV)

⁴¹But the Lord answered her, "Martha, Martha, you are worried and distracted by many things; ⁴²there is need of only one thing. Mary has chosen the better part, which will not be taken away from her."

Are you one of those people who can't watch TV when the kitchen is a mess or can't do your homework without a certain song or pen?

Is your room a mess right now?

What happens when following Jesus conflicts with our "other" life in the "real world"?

Read John 11:29–32.

When was the last time you wanted something so badly that you could not imagine not getting it?

Read John 12:1–3.

Is buying a new outfit for the dead person at a funeral a waste of money? Why or why not?

Matthew 27:55–56 (ASV).

⁵⁵And many women were there beholding from afar, who had followed Jesus from Galilee, ministering unto him: ⁵⁶among whom was Mary Magdalene, and Mary the mother of James and Joses, and the mother of the sons of Zebedee.

Could you hold your best friend's hand as your friend slowly died in a hospital room?

Could you hold the hand of a complete stranger as the person died at the scene of an accident?

When Jesus was dying many of the scriptures have the disciples running off and hiding while the women stayed till the end. Do you think women are generally stronger emotionally? Give an example.

How do you grieve?

John 20:16 (NRSV)

16Jesus said to her, "Mary!" She turned and said to him in Hebrew, "Rabbouni!" (which means Teacher).

Mary had no idea Jesus was standing behind her until he called her by name. Have you ever been oblivious to something amazing around you? Did you say "thank you" for the sunrise this morning?

Go back to Table Notes and erase the qualifications you wrote down. Write in your name instead. That's all you need to be.

Take Home Bag

One of the Marys purchased a jar of perfume. It was very expensive. She broke the jar and used it to clean Jesus' feet. That way the perfume's only purpose was Jesus.

Option 1: If you are in a coffee shop, check your
pockets and wallets. Pool your money and purchase the most expensive thing on the menu. Then turn around and give it away to the person in line behind. Say, "Have a nice day," and walk out.

Option 2: Pool your pocket money and give it to the youth leader. Decide on a place to purchase a gift card, and put this on the sexton's desk next week. (Leaving a note is not allowed.)

Tip

If they're going to write a story, they're going to write the story whether it's true or not.

—Mary Kate Olsen

LET'S GET READY TO RUMBLE

Theme: JACOB

Order Here

Remember Isaac from a few Explorations ago, the one who in the end didn't have to be sacrificed by his father? Jacob was one of Isaac's sons. Jacob was one of those guys who, metaphorically speaking, went a long way away and then had to come a long way back. He tricked his twin brother out of the family inheritance. Ran away rather than face his brother. Was tricked into marrying the sister of the woman he loved. Married the woman he loved anyway. Lied to a king. Wrestled with an angel. Patched things up with his brother and had a whole lot of children, including one who paraded around in a coat of many colors. His daughter was raped. His sons took revenge on an entire town. He had a well named after him, from which Jesus later drank.

Start Thinking

Choose one. I am...

- More of a listener/ talker.
- More contemplative/ action oriented.
- Patient / rash.
- Cynical / understanding.
- Willing to do whatever it takes /...as long as no one get hurt.
- A person who waits for guidance / a person who learns from my mistakes.
- A person who will sacrifice for the greater good / a person who will sacrifice *you* for the greater good.

- A person who has a good sense of my place in the grand scheme of things / a person who barely knows my own name most days.
- A person who is aware of God's continuous presence in my life /... God? Hellllooooo? Me again? God?

TABLE NOTES

Much of Jacob's story and his own philosophy deals with his covenant with God. It is a covenant that God makes for Jacob and all his descendants. Imagine that you are going to get a tattoo that you feel symbolizes your connection with God. It is a tattoo that all your children and grandchildren will get as well. Draw it here, in your journal, or on another piece of paper.

SCRIPTURE MENU

Look up the verses and ask the questions that follow.

Jacob's life is marked by four separate encounters with God. Each one was a "game-changer" for Jacob and his family, as you'll read in these stories.

Genesis 28:12
Jacob saw a "stairway to heaven" in his vision. In some translations it's a ladder and in others it's more of a staircase carved into a mountain, with angels walking up and down the stairs between heaven and earth. Some interpret this vision as a sign of God's presence on earth. Some say it is simply a sign that all life has its up and downs (Jacob's sure did). Some Christians believe that the ladder was Jesus and that the dream was a symbol of the "only way" to heaven.

Have you ever had a very powerful dream that you still remember and wish you could figure out what it means? What do you think a "stairway between heaven and earth" would mean if you saw it in your dream? Interpret the idea of such a stairway or ladder personally, and then as if it were a global message.

Jacob has this dream right after he tricks his own brother out of the family inheritance. God confers his blessing on Jacob. Does this mean God approves of Jacob's actions? Why or why not?

Genesis 31:12–13

The same way that Jacob manipulated his brother, Rachel's father Laban manipulated Jacob. But Jacob sticks around for fourteen years so that he can marry Rachel. Then God says, "Okay, you can go now." Do you think God would hold you back? Have you ever been so frustrated by your situation that you wanted to scream and then found out later that maybe it was a good thing you didn't run headlong into the situation? Talk about that.

Notice that God essentially said, "I know what you've been going through." If God were to say that to you, would you think, "Why didn't you do something about it before now?" Or would you take comfort in that idea? Explain.

It's also interesting to note that the Jacob was not the same man who first encountered God after leaving his family. Imagine yourself as an eight-year old. Could that eight-year old have handled your life as it is now?

Is the saying "Whatever doesn't kill you makes you stronger" true? Is God making you stronger right now? Any idea what for? Would you want to know?

Genesis 32:24–28 (NRSV)

24 Jacob was left alone; and a man wrestled with him until daybreak. 25 When the man saw that he did not prevail against Jacob, he struck him on the hip socket; and Jacob's hip was put out of joint as he wrestled with him. 26 Then he said, "Let me go, for the day is breaking." But Jacob said, "I will not let you go, unless you bless me." 27 So he said to him, "What is your name?" And he said, "Jacob." 28 Then the man said, "You shall no longer be called Jacob, but Israel, for you have striven with God and with humans, and have prevailed."

In the third stage, Jacob was in a new role as a grabber. This time, by the Jordan River, he grabbed on to God and wouldn't let go. God achieved a firm hold on him. In responding to Joseph's invitation to come to Egypt, Jacob was clearly unwilling to make a move without God's approval.

The ancient Jews believed that certain areas of the body controlled certain emotions. Love, for example, was not controlled by the heart but by the stomach. Pride was in the pelvic area. Jacob's hipbone (his pride) had to be dislocated before he could meet his brother. Is there anything about you that probably should be "dislocated" before you can move on with the next part of your life?

Genesis 46:2–4

Jacob has been through incredible hardships, and God is reassuring him saying, "Don't worry." God also tells Jacob that the son he thought was dead will be there by his bedside when he dies. Which do you think is better, to leave behind the broken pieces of your life or to have them all brought back and put together?

Notice in Genesis 32:1–2 that God meets Jacob where he is. God doesn't make Jacob become someone new and *then* meets him. God meets Jacob where he is now.

TAKE HOME BAG

If we say there are four different Jacobs, which one is most like you right now at this time in your life? Note—one is not necessarily better than other. You might be in-between somewhere. You might be on your way out of one phase and into another. Where do you think you are?

1. The runner—making God come and find you
2. The waiter—waiting for God to say "stay" or "go"
3. The wrestler—fighting with God every step of the way
4. The present—happy to have God meet you where you are

 TIP

There's a sign on the wall
But she wants to be sure
'Cause you know sometimes words have two meanings.

—Led Zeppelin, "Stairway to Heaven"

GUT WRENCHING (ACTS 1:18)

THEME: JUDAS

5

ORDER HERE

Judas was one of the most puzzling figures of the Gospels and his actions often create more questions than answers. He was chosen to be one of Christ's disciples, yet he betrayed Jesus. Why would anyone do such a thing? Was he following God's plan? Did Jesus know this was going to happen? Is that the sole reason Judas was chosen? Because of Judas' actions, we had the resurrection, the very cornerstone of our faith. Why is Judas not celebrated? In this Exploration, we won't answer any of these questions, but we will try to talk about them and perhaps get a little closer to understanding one of the most hated men in history.

START THINKING

Choose one.

- Adapt to the situation / Change the situation
- Give a man a fish / Teach a man to fish
- I like the feeling of a fat wallet. / I always feel guilty when I see homeless people.
- Snooze you lose / Wait your turn
- Heal the bird's broken wing. / Put it out of its misery.
- Sometimes force is necessary. / Diplomacy, diplomacy, diplomacy
- There are long-range answers to consider. / Fix the problem, then deal with the outcome.

TABLE NOTES

In the space below or on a napkin or the back of a place mat, create an original bumper sticker for a cause you truly believe in.

Would you be willing to put these all over your city? Would you risk getting arrested to do so? Would you go to jail for this cause if you were asked to?

SCRIPTURE MENU

Look up one or more of the sets of verses, and respond to the discussion questions that follow.

There's a classic Batman comic in which Superman gives Batman the only known piece of kryptonite. Batman is apparently the one person Superman trusts to "do what should be done" in case it's necessary. The book *The Gospel of Judas*, published a few years ago, seems to indicate a similar relationship—that Judas was the one person Jesus could trust with the plan. Could you "do what needs to be done" if it meant you would lose everything and be hated for the rest of time by all generations?

Mark 9:32 (MontgomeryNT)
But they did not understand his words, and were afraid to ask him the meaning.

Luke 2:50 (MontgomeryNT)
But they did not understand the words that he spoke to them.

Luke 9:45 (NRSV)
But they did not understand this saying; its meaning was concealed from them, so that they could not perceive it. And they were afraid to ask him about this saying.

John 8:27 (NRSV)
They did not understand that he was speaking to them about the Father.

John 12:16 (NRSV)
His disciples did not understand these things at first; but when Jesus was glorified, then they remembered that these things had been written of him and had been done to him.

These are just a few verses that seem to indicate that most if not all of the disciples didn't have a clue what Jesus was talking about. Have you ever sat through a class where you had no idea what was going on? Judas joined up with Jesus thinking that the "new kingdom" was physical, that Jesus was going to overthrow the government. Can we fault him for not getting the message when no one else did either?

When Judas was chosen as a disciple, the gospels of Matthew, Mark, and Luke all say Judas was "the one who betrayed him."

Acts 1:17 (MsgB)
Judas was one of us and had his assigned place in this ministry.

Do you think this was Judas' assigned role in history? If this really was God's plan from the beginning, then wasn't Judas following God's plan in a way that many of us could never do?

John 13:27–30 (NRSV)
[27]After he received the piece of bread, Satan entered into him. Jesus said to him, "Do quickly what you are going to do." [28]Now no one at the table knew why he said this to him. [29]Some thought that, because Judas had the common purse, Jesus was telling him, "Buy what we need for the festival"; or, that he should give

something to the poor. ³⁰So, after receiving the piece of bread, he immediately went out. And it was night.

In John's gospel, Judas does not eat the bread he is given. The ritual of communion is about taking Christ into ourselves and becoming "one" with him. Do you think John put this detail in on purpose? In what ways do we "ignore the bread" in our own lives?

TAKE HOME BAG

Write down one thing that has always puzzled you about Jesus Christ. It can be anything you want. Write it here.

Chances are Judas asked that same question. This week say a few prayers and ask God to give you understanding.

Is Judas in heaven?

Couldn't believe, couldn't believe
How you deceived, you deceived.
I never thought you'd do that to me.

—*Kelly Clarkson, "Judas"*

LIKE A ROLLING STONE

THEME: PETER

ORDER HERE

Have you ever watched a video online where someone tries something really, really stupid like jumping off a building or trying to do something on a skateboard off a house? There will be people who look at that and say, "What an idiot." But there is always one who says, "Coooool."

Peter is the one who would try it just to see if it was possible. Peter was probably the disciple who could have benefited from a good dose of ritalin. He was brash and impulsive. He usually spoke before he thought. But when he, in effect, took over the ministry from Jesus, he became an impassioned leader. He shared the message with the same joy you'd see if you gave an eight-year-old a water balloon.

START THINKING

Choose one. Which is closer to your life philosophy?

- Don't do that—you'll poke your eye out. / Geronimooooo.
- Mild sauce, please. / Do you have anything hotter?
- Sugar-Free Gum / Caffeine is my friend.
- Extra cheese / Do you have any more pineapple?
- Jesus sat alone and prayed. / Jesus stood up and calmed a storm! How cool is that?

- Use your inside voice. / LET'S GET READY TO RUMMMMMMBLLLLE!
- I've never been to the hospital. / They know my face in the emergency room.
- Hammer and nails / Air compressor and nail gun...AND A TARGET!

TABLE NOTES

Based on what you know about Peter, create a bumper sticker you might see on the back of his car.

SCRIPTURE MENU

Look up one or more of the sets of verses, and respond to the discussion questions that follow.

Acts 2:14–15(NRSV)

14But Peter, standing with the eleven, raised his voice and addressed them: "Men of Judea and all who live in Jerusalem, let this be known to you, and listen to what I say. 15Indeed, these are not drunk, as you suppose, for it is only nine o'clock in the morning."

What subject do you love to talk about—the one thing that when you start down the path your friends roll their eyes and say, "Here we go again"?

What do you notice about the people who love the subject they are talking about? Have you ever watched comedian Lewis Black speak? What do you notice most?

Read these next three passages and then look at the questions.

Matthew 4:18–20 (NRSV)

18As he walked by the Sea of Galilee, he saw two brothers, Simon, who is called Peter, and Andrew his brother, casting a net into the lake—for they were fishermen. 19And he said to them, "Follow me, and I will make you fish for people." 20Immediately they left their nets and followed him.

Matthew 14:28–31 (NRSV)

²⁸Peter answered him, "Lord, if it is you, command me to come to you on the water." ²⁹He said, "Come." So Peter got out of the boat, started walking on the water, and came towards Jesus. ³⁰But when he noticed the strong wind, he became frightened, and beginning to sink, he cried out, "Lord, save me!" ³¹Jesus immediately reached out his hand and caught him, saying to him, "You of little faith, why did you doubt?"

John 21:7 (MsgB)

Then the disciple Jesus loved said to Peter, "It's the Master!" When Simon Peter realized that it was the Master, he threw on some clothes, for he was stripped for work, and dove into the sea.

Do you have a friend who if you pulled up while the friend was doing yard work and said, "Let's go," your friend would simply drop the rake and get in the car? How do these people get through life? How do they keep from getting in trouble?

Peter stepped out of the boat when no one else did. He also sank like a stone. There were eleven other guys in the boat. Do you think they gave him a hard time for sinking?

If you did three or four steps on the water and then nearly drowned, would you be jazzed about the steps or freaked about the near drowning?

In the John reading, Peter puts his clothes <ital>on<> and then jumps in the water. What "crazy" friend of yours would do something like that?

What are the benefits of acting before you think? What about thinking it through first?

Read Acts 4:13–14.

What adult do you know who was probably a lunatic when he or she was a teenager? Does that spark ever go out? Is it true that people either mature or go into youth ministry?

Read Acts 11:4–10.

Peter was constantly learning and exploring his faith. Peter tried to say, "No thanks. I'm on a religious diet." God said, "Who are you to say that what I make isn't any good?" What is the greater symbolism here? In our culture, who is on the sheet?

Read Acts 12:5–11.

Does it seem like those who are willing to risk bruises and bones somehow get protected? Do guardian angels work over time for some people? Is it hard to be around people who always seem to get by on luck?

The Internet is full of people whose last words should be, "Hey guys, watch this." Yet they always seem to survive. How could you apply that attitude to your faith?

Matthew 16:18 (NRSV)
And I tell you, you are Peter, and on this rock I will build my church, and the gates of Hades will not prevail against it.

If this is the kind of person that Peter is—and Jesus says, "I'm making you the cornerstone of the church" (metaphorically speaking), what was Jesus calling for church to look like? How are we doing so far?

Take Home Bag

Let's go back to Peter's car. On the back of a place mat or on another sheet of paper, draw a street sign you think represents Peter's faith. Rip that out and put it in your wallet or tape it to your mirror. Pray this week and ask God to show you how you can share the message in your own way.

Share with a friend or parent an online video you've seen that could represent the brashness and impulsiveness of Peter's faith—"Hey guys, watch this..."

COAT RACK

THEME: PAUL

ORDER HERE

Forget that Paul wrote a chunk of the New Testament. Put that aside and look at the life he lived—shipwrecks, snake bite, prison breaks, a full-contact encounter with God's pointer finger. You couldn't make this into a movie because no one would believe this was one of God's main guys, especially since Paul started out by being the coat holder while one of the other disciples was stoned to death.

This Exploration will focus not so much on the writings of Paul but on the life events that inspired those writings.

START THINKING

True or False?

- If it's too loud, you're too old.
- "It's better to burn out than to fade away." (Neil Young)
- "Rock and roll music—the music of freedom frightens people and unleashes all manner of conservative defense mechanisms." (Salman Rushdie)
- "People should be ecstatic and cry at the same time." (Wayne Coyne)
- "People, whether they know it or not, like their blues singers miserable. They like their blues singers to die afterwards." (Janis Joplin)
- "I'd rather be hated for who I am than loved for who I am not." (Kurt Cobain)

TABLE NOTES

Think about some of your favorite action movies. There's often a standard character off to the side—the wiser guy who's a tough old bird. He survives the accidents and can look you in the eye while he pulls the arrow out of his shoulder and laughs. See how many "tough old bird" characters you can come up with.

SCRIPTURE MENU

Have someone look up the verses and ask the questions aloud.

Acts 7:57–58

⁵⁷But they covered their ears, and with a loud shout all rushed together against him. ⁵⁸Then they dragged him out of the city and began to stone him; and the witnesses laid their coats at the feet of a young man named Saul.

This was when Stephen, one of the leaders of the church after Jesus came back, was stoned to death for preaching the word of Christ. People said, "Here sonny, hold my coat." Paul (whose name was Saul at the time) stood there and held people's cloaks while they stoned Stephen to death. Could you hold the executioner's coffee while he pushed the button to execute a child molester? What if it were a radical terrorist suspect who'd been arrested but not convicted by law?

Acts 9:1–9 (MsgB)

All this time Saul was breathing down the necks of the Master's disciples, out for the kill. He went to the Chief Priest and got arrest warrants to take to the meeting places in Damascus so that if he found anyone there belonging to the Way, whether men or women, he could arrest them and bring them to Jerusalem.

He set off. When he got to the outskirts of Damascus, he was suddenly dazed by a blinding flash of light. As he fell to the ground, he heard a voice: "Saul, Saul, why are you out to get me?"

He said, "Who are you, Master?"

"I am Jesus, the One you're hunting down. I want you to get up and enter the city. In the city you'll be told what to do next."

His companions stood there dumbstruck—they could hear the sound, but couldn't see anyone—while Saul, picking himself up off the ground, found himself stone blind. They had to take him by the hand and lead him into Damascus. He continued blind for three days. He ate nothing, drank nothing.

This was Paul's big conversion. He was a jerk who would hunt down Christians and put them in jail. Then one day God reaches down and flicks him off his horse, blinding him.

When Saul said, "Who are you?" the voice said, "I am Jesus, the One you're hunting down."

Assuming this was Jesus' voice, what do you think he meant by that sentence? The King James translation also tells us that Jesus said, "It is hard for thee to kick against the pricks." This was a phrase that referred to the way a farm ox would kick when the farmer poked it with a sharp stick. Jesus is telling Paul, "You're not so tough now, are you?"

Why don't some people listen until they get smacked upside the head? When have you been one of those? What lesson did you not get until someone dope slapped you?

Have you ever known someone or seen someone on television and wished God would reach down and just thump that person a good one? Think of the nastiest person you know, and imagine you hear that God finally did something about him or her...and then you hear that God made the person a minister. How would you feel?

If Osama bin Laden showed up and said, "God spoke to me and wants me to tell you that Jesus loves you," how long would he last? Do you think there would be any Christian churches that would say, "Welcome"? What would your church do?

Read Acts 9:17–18.

Imagine the impossible event from the last discussion question has occurred—Osama bin Laden has showed up. Now God speaks to you, right there in your high school, and says, "Go talk to him. Tell him I sent you." Would you go? If God called you to prison ministry, would you go?

Read Acts 28:3–6.

This sounds like Paul as played by Vin Diesel or Arnold Schwarzenegger. God chose this moment to show the people that this man was indeed one of his servants. The people around automatically think he's a God.

What is hero worship? How guilty of it are we in our culture? Do you think it happens in other cultures? Can you think of the last time our country held up a hero and then forgot about that hero when the next one came along?

Read Acts 16:22–26.

Today, what song would you sing? What would be the most appropriate song?

Read Acts 21:31–36, 22:22–25, 23:10.

The crowd is prepared to yank Paul's arms and legs from their sockets and let him bleed to death. The Bible doesn't say Paul panicked or screamed in fear. He simply seemed to turn and say, "Uh...excuse me...is this legal?" Paul was using his wits to get out of the situation. Who do you know that would best be able to keep his or her head in a crisis?

At what point do you think you would have turned around and gone home? Paul gets into these situations one after the other and yet seems to have no fear. If you take away the "fear" or someone's ability to make you afraid, what do you take from that person?

Acts 26:24 (NRSV)
While he was making this defense, Festus exclaimed, "You are out of your mind, Paul! Too much learning is driving you insane!"

Be honest, how many times have you heard something like *that*? Isn't this something you generally outgrow? Do you know any adult who still needs to hear this once in awhile? Is this a good thing or a bad thing?

TAKE HOME BAG

This week go home and find a quotation. Let it be the most defiant, in-your-face line ever spoken by one person to a greater authority. Memorize it and bring it with you to the next meeting.

TIP

All that's left now is the shouting...

—Paul, in 2 Timothy 4:8 (MsgB)

TELL ME, WHOSE WRITIN' IS THIS?

Theme: JOHN THE REVELATOR

Order Here

Revelation is probably one of the most widely interpreted books and wildly *misinterpreted* books ever written. No doubt there is someone in your generation who pronounces knowledge of the secrets to Gog and Magog and can tell you who the Antichrist is or will be. Trouble is, your grandparents probably could do the same thing for their generation. In this Exploration, we will not even attempt to sort out the vision seen by John. Instead, we will look at the writer himself, and in getting to know the writer perhaps we can get a better understanding of the writing.

Start Thinking

Choose one. Which of these pairs does not exist in the book of Revelation?

- Slaughtered Lamb's Book of Life / Fire-breathing dragons
- A "beast" with seven heads / One beast using another beast as a puppet
- The Mother of whores and other abominations / A star named Wormwood
- An eagle that screams "Doom Doom Doom" / A trumpet that kills everything that lives in the sea
- A white horse with a pale rider / A book that, when eaten, tastes good but makes you sick

(Trick questions—they all appear in Revelation.)

TABLE NOTES

In the space below or on the back of a place mat or napkin, draw a number seven. Make it as "complete" as you can. Be creative. Show perspective. Draw details. You can draw it made out of jelly beans or diamonds, or draw it like a seven-shaped frosted donut. Just make it a "complete" seven.

SCRIPTURE MENU

Look up one or more of the sets of verses, and respond to the discussion questions that follow.

There are several ways to view the book of Revelation.

1. John was writing to people of his own day, offering encouragement to those who knew they would die in slavery, as had their ancestors, as would their descendents. Using a code, John wrote that eventually it would all turn upside down and the slaves would be the masters.
2. John had a vision of the "end times." This was a prophecy of how it would all end.
3. John's writing was more historical—an allegory about the continuous struggle of his people. The names may change but the story does not.
4. John's book was a symbolic story about Good vs. Evil.

   Because the book is so widely interpreted, the question we need to ask ourselves is this: How do the writings of John make me a better Christian? No matter which way you see the book, the question still applies.

Amos 3:7 (NRSV)
**Surely the Lord God does nothing,
without revealing his secret
to his servants the prophets.**

John 16:12 (NRSV)
**"I still have many things to say to you, but you cannot bear
them now."**

Galatians 1:11–12 (NRSV)
**[11]For I want you to know, brothers and sisters, that the gospel
that was proclaimed by me is not of human origin; [12]for I did not
receive it from a human source, nor was I taught it, but I received
it through a revelation of Jesus Christ.**

John 15:15 (NRSV)
**"I do not call you servants any longer, because the servant does
not know what the master is doing; but I have called you friends,
because I have made known to you everything that I have heard
from my Father."**

A "revelation" by biblical definition is when God reveals something that was previously unknown. The last four scripture passages seem to indicate that God makes a habit of this. Could the younger version of you have understood the concept of God that the current version of you holds?

When was the last time something was "revealed" to you about your life or family, something that was previously unknown and then suddenly you hear it and say, "Are you *serious*?!! I never knew that before?"

When was the last time something was "revealed" to you about God? Who revealed it to you? What were the circumstances?

John was sitting in a cave on the island of Patmos when he wrote Revelation. He was exiled to this island with other "criminals" to work in a mine. John makes it plain that the revelation came on a Sabbath day.

Revelation 1:4–5 (NRSV)
**[4]John to the seven churches that are in Asia:
    Grace to you and peace from him who is and who was and who
is to come, and from the seven spirits who are before his throne,
[5]and from Jesus Christ, the faithful witness, the firstborn of the**

dead, and the ruler of the kings of the earth.

In scripture, the number seven is symbolic. It refers to completeness. So, biblical farmers would divide their lands into seven parts; and when Jesus is asked about how many times we should forgive someone he says, "Seventy times seven" (which means infinitely, not 490). In referring to Seven Spirits, John means the "complete spirit"—the Holy Spirit.

What gives you a feeling of "completeness" in your life? Have you ever known someone who never seems to feel complete? What about a person who seems more complete than most people? What do they do to feel this way?

John describes himself as a follower of Christ, an eyewitness to Christ, a spiritual leader in the world, a servant of angels, and a brother of prophets. Why would God allow a person who was all these things to languish in an island prison?

Read Revelation 22:18–19.

These are the words John uses to close the book. How does this work with the way people interpret the book of Revelation? Have you ever heard someone "add" or "take away" words from the Bible? How do we twist the meaning of the scriptures to meet our own needs?

Take Home Bag

This week remind yourself to pay attention to what people **aren't** saying. What do they reveal to the world through actions, writings, clothing, and other nonverbal communications? Keep a list, and bring it with you to the next gathering.

Tip

Jesus said, "I am coming soon." Given that it's been two thousand years, why hasn't he shown up yet?

—Ken Smith, in **Ken's Guide to the Bible**

EXPLORATION

18

AFTERWORD:
HOW TO USE THIS BOOK

This book was born out of a conversation with a friend of mine at a large church in the central United States. She said that her church was going to do away with the traditional Sunday night meetings because of low attendance. They would keep Sunday morning as well as the Wednesday night Bible study. "The thing is," she said, "I still have fifty kids in and out of my office during the week, and it's not necessarily the same kids. What I need is a curriculum that requires no preparation—and that I can grab off my shelf, take four youth, and say 'Let's go over to Starbucks.'"

This book works two ways. The first is as an impromptu discussion starter to be used with five or less youth crammed into a booth at your favorite coffee shop or diner. The participants can write on place mats or napkins. Just you, a Bible (or a few, different versions), and a couple of pens, and you're ready to go.

You can also use this book as part of an on-going curriculum. If possible, give each participant his or her own copy of this book to write in and doodle on as a journal. If youth are sharing copies, it would be great if each youth could get his or her own journal, one that's small enough to fit into a book bag and be re-read or worked on at home.

Adapt It Up
Every youth worker has opened a book of games or discussions only to be faced with the first line, "Break your group into smaller groups of eight"—and you have a total of only six teens in the room. We've all had to "adapt it down" and try to make a large-group activity fit with a small group. This book is written so that a youth minister or Sunday school teacher can adapt it *up* for use with a larger group.

How to Use This Book
Each exploration is broken into six smaller sections. The activities can be followed sequentially or not.

Order Here
This is the introduction. You can read it aloud to your youth, or, if each has his or her own book, you can have them read along silently before moving on.

Start Thinking
These are quick focusing questions to get kids' brains in the proper mindset and the discussion moving. They are mostly fun questions, meant to start things off. There are no right or wrong answers, so pay attention to the responses. If possible, ask more questions based on the answers you receive. These answers will give you a good idea of where the discussion wants to go.

Table Notes

This section encourages active participation. Youth are asked to make lists, draw pictures, and so on. Make sure they know they don't have to be artists or poets to properly participate. Sometimes discussion is easier if your hands are busy, so encourage doodling—yes, in the books! The idea is to get teens to open up and talk about what they are thinking.

Scripture Menu

Encourage your youth to bring their own Bibles. Tell them they can go out and buy a translation that speaks to them (the more variety, the better). Be open to the idea of letting participants mark and write in their Bibles—to really use the books.

This section offers up several different scriptures. Use as many as you want. Each scripture reference is followed by one, two, or several discussion questions. This time may be when you have the deepest discussion and when participants may start asking their own questions. Pay attention to these and follow their logic—this book should be merely the starting point for deeper things. The goal is to help youth learn who they are and what they think and believe, and then to share that with others.

Take Home Bag

This section is a work-at-home assignment. If your participants each have their own books, this will be easier. If they don't, let them write down the assignment on the back of a place mat or napkin. If you are using this book as part of a regular gathering, tell participants that they don't have to share their answers unless they are comfortable doing so.

Tip

The tip is a quick "big idea" for the day, like a fortune in a cookie or the memorable quote on the side of the paper coffee cup. Encourage participants to see the tip as a life hint and to pay attention to how often it comes into play during the week.

The questions in this book have been around for ages. They are part of an attempt to explain our place in the universe. They are also questions that have inflamed many arguments and caused great schisms and separations in families and churches. It has been said that the job of the clergy is not to answer the questions but to protect them. Some things we won't know about God until we can pose the question face to face. In the meantime, this book is written to create discussion. If you don't come to a conclusion...just enjoy the ride.

Everyone likes to work with little kids. Their hugs are freely given, and they act like they are glad to see you. Finding leaders for the adult education program is a little harder, mostly because adults don't think they're smart enough to lead a Bible discussion. In adult classes you can have adult discussions, but you have chosen to work with teenagers. God bless you. I hope these books make you even better at what you do.